The Crazy Joke Book

From admirals to zebra crossings, there's
a joke for every occasion in this book.
'Knock-knocks', puns, crazy book titles,
daft definitions and schoolboy howlers all
make an appearance, and there's a good
selection of the funniest 'waiter' jokes,
'doctor' jokes and 'schoolteacher' jokes.

THE CRAZY JOKE BOOK

Compiled by Janet Rogers

Illustrated by Robert Nixon,
Graham Thompson and John Smyth

Beaver Books

First published in 1979 by
The Hamlyn Publishing Group Limited
London · New York · Sydney · Toronto
Astronaut House, Feltham, Middlesex, England
Sixth impression 1982

© Copyright Text Victorama Limited 1979
© Copyright Illustrations
The Hamlyn Publishing Group Limited 1979
ISBN 0 600 35270 6

Typeset, printed and bound in Great Britain by
Hazell Watson & Viney Limited
Aylesbury, Bucks
Set in Intertype Times

Contents

Introduction

This book is just like the lady the magician saws in half. It comes in two parts. The first part is an incredible dictionary of jokes. The second part is an incredible joke dictionary. What's the difference between the two? Read the book and you'll find out. And if you can't read, don't worry. The book is still useful. Find a wobbly table or chair in your house and wedge the book under it!

J. R.

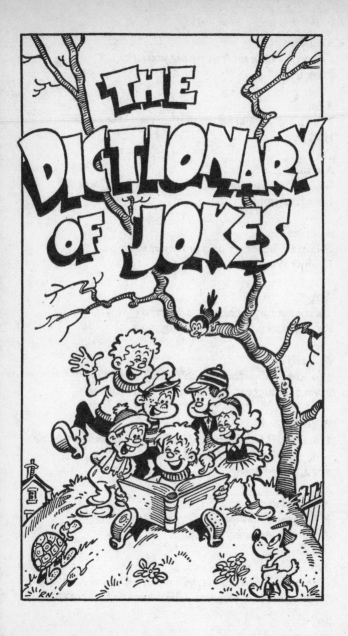

Acoustics
The acoustics in this theatre are fantastic.
Pardon?

Admiral
What's higher than an admiral?
His hat.

Aircraft
What is big, hairy and flies to New York at 2250 kph?
King Kongcorde.

Ancestors
One of my ancestors died at Waterloo.
Really? Which platform?

Anger
FIRST MAN: *Why are you so angry?*
SECOND MAN: Oh, it's all the rage now.

Animals
TEACHER: *Name four animals of the cat family.*
PUPIL: Father cat, Mother cat, and two kittens.

Apples
TEACHER: *If I had forty apples in one hand and fifty in the other, what would I have?*
PUPIL: Big hands.

Archaeologist
What's the definition of an archaeologist?
A man whose career is in ruins.

Ark
What's the difference between Noah's Ark and Joan of Arc?
One was made of wood, and the other was Maid of Orleans.

Astronaut
What did the astronaut see in his frying-pan?
An unidentified frying object.

Astronauts
Where do astronauts leave their spaceships?
At parking meteors.

Athletics
What is the best diet for athletes?
Runner beans.

Atlantic
What do you get if you cross the Atlantic with the Titanic?
Halfway.

Attention
TEACHER : *I wish you'd pay a little attention.*
PUPIL : I'm paying as little as I can.

Audience
What's the difference between an angry audience and a cow with laryngitis?
One boos madly and the other moos badly.

Baby

How do you get a baby astronaut to sleep?
You rock-et.

Bad luck

When is it bad luck to have a black cat follow you?
When you are a mouse.

Baldness

Why is a bald man's head like Alaska?
It's a great white bear place.

Banana

What do you do if you find a blue banana?
Try to cheer it up.

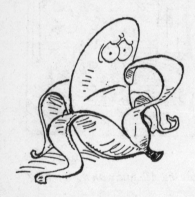

Band

CUSTOMER: *Will the band play anything I request?*
WAITER: Certainly, sir.
CUSTOMER: *Tell them to play cards.*

Barber

BARBER: *Were you wearing a red scarf when you came in?*
CUSTOMER: No.
BARBER: *Oh! Then I must have cut your throat.*

Bath
Why did the bank robber take a bath?
So he could make a clean getaway.

Bears
Why do bears have fur coats?
Because they would look stupid in plastic macs.

Beaver
What did the beaver say to the tree?
It was nice gnawing you.

Bed
Why do people go to bed?
Because the bed won't come to them.

Bed
Shall I tell you the joke about the bed?
No, it hasn't been made yet.

Beehive
Why is a beehive like a rotten potato?
A beehive is a bee-holder, and a beholder is a spectator,
    and a specked tater is a rotten potato.

Beer
A barrel of beer fell on a man. Why wasn't he hurt?
It was light ale.

Bees
Why do bees hum?
Because they don't know the words.

Bell
What did the bell say when it fell in the water?
I'm wringing wet.

Birthday presents
What's the best birthday present?
Difficult question, but a drum takes a lot of beating.

Bison
What is the difference between a buffalo and a bison?
You can't wash your hands in a buffalo.

Bite
How do you find out where a flea has bitten you?
Start from scratch.

Blacksmith
The judge found the blacksmith guilty of forging.

Boating
Come in, Number 9. Your time is up.
But we've only got eight boats.
Are you in trouble, Number 6?

Bongos
INTERVIEWER: *Excuse my asking, but what are those tiny little bongos hanging from your ears?*
PUNK-STAR: Oh, they're just my ear-drums.

Bow
What kind of bow is impossible to tie?
A rainbow.

Brain
What's the cure for water on the brain?
A tap on the head.

Breakfast
What do ghosts have for breakfast?
Dreaded Wheat.

Broom
Why does a witch ride on a broom?
A vacuum cleaner is too heavy.

Brother
My brother thinks he's a chicken. We'd take him to the
   doctor but we can't do without the eggs.

Budgerigars
What is the best time to buy budgies?
When they are going cheap.

Bull
What did the bull say to the cow?
When I fall in love it will be for heifer.

Burglar
*What did the burglar say to the lady of the house when she
   caught him stealing her silver?*
I am at your service, Ma'am.

Burial
*Why didn't they bury the Duke of Wellington with full
   military honours in 1847?*
Because he didn't die until 1852.

Butcher

WOMAN: *I want a nice piece of bacon. And make it lean.*
BUTCHER: Which way, madam?

Butterfly

Why couldn't the butterfly get into the dance?
Because it was a moth-ball.

Cabbages

There were two parallel lines of cabbages, so the farmer called it a dual cabbage way.

Cakes

What jumps from cake to cake and tastes of almonds?
Tarzipan.

Candles

Candles make light meals.

Cannibal

Do you like beans?
Yes, very much.
What sort do you like eating best?
Human bein's.

Car
I recently bought a baby car – it doesn't go anywhere
   without a rattle.

Cards
Why is it dangerous to play cards in the jungle?
Because of all the cheetahs.

Cat
What noise does a cat make going down the M1?
Miaoooooooooooooooooooooooooow!

Cats
What do cats read every morning?
Mewspapers.

Charge
POLICEMAN: *I'm afraid that I'm going to have to lock you
   up for the night.*
MAN: What's the charge?
POLICEMAN: *Oh, there's no charge. It's all part of the
   service.*

Chemist
CUSTOMER: *Chemist, I'd like some poison for mice.*
CHEMIST: Have you tried Boots?
CUSTOMER: *I want to poison them – not kick them to death.*

Chess
My dog plays chess with me.
That's amazing! It must be a really intelligent animal.
Not really. I've won three games to two so far this evening.

Chickens
Who tells chicken jokes?
Comedihens.

Children
What children live in the sea?
Buoys and gulls.

Chops
CUSTOMER: *Waiter! This chop is very tough.*
WAITER: Yes, sir, it's probably a karate chop.
CUSTOMER: *Well, have you got pig's trotters?*
WAITER: No, sir – flat feet.

Cinema
CINEMA ATTENDANT: *That's the sixth ticket you've bought.*
CUSTOMER: Yes, I know, there's a girl in there that keeps tearing them up.

Circle
Why were seven wooden planks standing in a circle?
They were having a board meeting.

Citrus fruits
How do you help deaf citrus fruits?
Give them a lemon aid.

Cleaning
Why did the cleaning woman stop cleaning?
Because she found grime doesn't pay.

Cobbler
What did the cobbler say when a flock of chickens came into his workshop?
Shoo!

Cock-a-doodle-do
What is the opposite of Cock-a-doodle-do?
Cock-a-doodle-don't.

Coffee

CUSTOMER: *Waiter! This coffee tastes like mud.*

WAITER: Well, sir, it was ground only ten minutes ago.

Containers

Can an orange box?

No, but a tomato can.

Cooks

Why are cooks cruel?

They beat eggs, whip cream and batter fish.

Cow

I say, what a lovely colour that cow over there is.

It's a Jersey.

Really? I thought it was her skin.

Cowboy

Who has eight guns and terrorises the ocean?

Billy the Squid.

Cowboys

FIRST COWBOY: *Did you know they call you 'Paleface' on the reservation?*

SECOND COWBOY: No – why's that?

FIRST COWBOY: *Because you've got a face like a bucket.*

Croak
What goes croak! croak! when it's misty?
A frog-horn.

Crocodile
What's a crocodile's favourite game?
Snap.

Cruelty
Why is a farmer cruel?
Because he pulls the corn by its ears.

Curtains
PATIENT: *Doctor, Doctor, I feel like a pair of curtains*
DOCTOR: Well, pull yourself together then.

Dancing
In one word, describe 154 dancing cakes.
Abundance.

Danger
What's green and highly dangerous?
A caterpillar with a machine gun.

December
What do you call a tug-of-war on December 24th?
Christmas 'Eave.

Dentist
MAN: *Give it me straight – how am I?*
DENTIST: Well, sir your teeth are all right – but I'm afraid
your gums will have to come out.

Detective
*What did the detective say when he tracked down the
crook?*
I'm policed to meet you.

Directions
MOTORIST: *Could you tell me the way to Bath?*
POLICEMAN: I always use soap and water.

Doctor
Why was the unemployed doctor angry?
Because he had no patients.

Dog
I've just lost my dog.
Why don't you put an advertisement in the paper?
Don't be silly – my dog can't read.

Dolphins
Dolphins are so intelligent that within only a few weeks of being in captivity they can train a man to stand on the very edge of their pool and throw them fish three times a day.

Doorbell
How do you use an Egyptian doorbell?
Toot-and-come-in.

Door knockers
What did they give the man who invented door knockers?
The No Bell Prize.

Dracula
Where is Dracula's office in America?
In the Vampire State Building.

Dress
CUSTOMER: *I would like to try on that dress in the window, please.*
ASSISTANT: I'm sorry, madam, you'll have to try it on in the changing-rooms like everybody else.

Ducks

What happens to ducks who fly upside down?
They quack up.

Dustbin

PATIENT: *Doctor, Doctor, I keep thinking I'm a dustbin.*
DOCTOR: Don't talk rubbish.

Dying

Why is a dying man like a cobbler?
Because he gives up his awl, looks to his end, and prepares
   his soul for the last.

Eggs

Have you heard the joke about the eggs?
No.
Two bad.

Elastic

Why is elastic one of the longest words in the dictionary?
Because it stretches.

Elections

What bird will never vote in an election?
A mynah bird, because he's too young.

Electrician

Why did the man become an electrician?
He was looking for a bit of light relief.

Electrician

*What did the electrician's wife say when he arrived home
   late?*
Wire you insulate?

Emergency

What happens when you dial 666?
A policeman comes along walking on his hands.

Eskimo

What do you call an Eskimo wearing five balaclavas?
Anything you like, because he can't hear you.

Excuses

TEACHER (on phone): *You say Johnny has a cold and can't come to school. To whom am I speaking?*
VOICE: This is my father.

Eye

JOE: *The police are looking for a man with one eye called Oscar McTavish.*
JIM: Oh, yes. And what's his other eye called?

Famous last words

At the inquest, the coroner gently asked the widow: 'Could you tell us what your late husband's last words were?'

'Yes,' she replied. 'He said: "I really don't see how they can make a profit out of selling this corned beef at ten pence a tin..."'

Fire
Who invented fire?
Oh, some bright spark.

Fireplace
Who invented the first fireplace?
Alfred the Grate.

Fir trees
What do sad fir trees do?
They pine a lot.

Fishermen
What is essential for deaf fishermen?
A herring aid.

Fjord
What is a Fjord?
A Norwegian motor car.

Fleas
How do you start a flea race?
One, two, flea . . . go!

Flies
How do you keep flies out of the kitchen?
Put a bucket of manure in the lounge.

Flowers
What did the big flower say to the little flower?
How are you, bud?

Flying squad
LADY TO POLICEMAN: Send for the flying squad, please, I've
lost my canary.

France

What is French, 305 metres high and wobbly?
The Trifle Tower.

Free speech

Do you believe in free speech?
I certainly do.
Good, can I use your telephone?

Frog

What's a frog's favourite sweet?
A lollihop.

Frogs' legs

CUSTOMER: *Waiter, have you got frog's legs?*
WAITER: No, sir, I always walk this way.

Garden

WOMAN: *You've been working in your garden for hours, what are you growing?*
GARDENER: Tired.

Geography

TEACHER: *Where are the Andes?*
PUPIL: At the end of my armies.

Geologists
Where do geologists put their samples?
In the rock-stacks.

Germs
Did you know that deep breathing kills germs?
Yes, but how do you get them to breathe deeply?

Giraffe
What do you get if you cross a giraffe with a dog?
An animal that barks at low-flying aircraft.

Gnomes
What do you feed under-nourished gnomes?
Elf-raising flour.

Goats
PATIENT: *Doctor, Doctor, I keep thinking I'm a goat.*
DOCTOR: How long have you had this feeling?
PATIENT: *Since I was a kid.*

Gold
How do you make gold soup?
Put fourteen carrots in it.

Green
What's green and slimy and goes hith?
A snake with a lisp.

Hair
Why do bees have sticky hair?
Because they have honey combs.

Hair
PATIENT: *My hair keeps falling out. Can you suggest anything to keep it in?*
DOCTOR: How about a carrier bag?

Hat
What did the hat say to the scarf?
You hang around while I go on ahead.

Hatstand
Why did the hatstand in the hall?
Because it had nowhere to sit.

Haute cuisine
MAN: *Waiter, can I have some horrible, greasy chips an underdone egg, and a steak that tastes like an old boot?*
WAITER: I'm sorry, sir, but we couldn't possibly give you anything like that.
MAN: *Why not? That's what you gave me yesterday.*

Health
What did the health attendant say to his girl assistant?
Hi, Jean.

Help

What sits in a fruit bowl and shouts for help?
A damson in distress.

Horse

What horse can't you ride?
A clothes horse.

Horse

Why has a horse got six legs?
Because he has forelegs in front and two legs behind.

Hotel

HOTEL MANAGER: *Well, sir, did you enjoy your stay here with us?*

GUEST: Yes, but I'm a bit upset about leaving the place so soon after I've practically bought it.

I

TEACHER: *Sue, say something beginning with 'I'.*

SUE: I is . . .

TEACHER: *No, Sue, you must say I am.*

SUE: All right, I am the ninth letter of the alphabet.

Igloo
What is an igloo?
An icicle made for two.

Illegal
What is meant by 'illegal'?
A sick bird of prey.

Invisible
PATIENT: *Doctor, Doctor, I keep thinking I'm invisible.*
DOCTOR: Who said that?

Jelly
What do you get when you cross a jelly with a sheep dog?
Collie-wobbles.

Jockey
Why did the jockey take hay to bed?
To feed his nightmares.

Judge
JUDGE: *Constable, do you recognise this woman?*
CONSTABLE: Yes, m'lud. She came up to me when I was in plain clothes and tried to pass this five-pound note off on me.
JUDGE: *Counterfeit?*
CONSTABLE: Yes, m'lud. She had two.

Judge
The judge was only four feet three inches tall – a small thing sent to try us.

Jungle
Why did an egg go into the jungle?

Because it was an eggsplorer.

Kangaroo
An Australian farmer tried to cross a kangaroo with a sheep
so he would get a woolly jumper.

Killing
Could you kill somebody just by throwing eggs at him?
Yes, he would be eggs-terminated.

Kitchen
DINER : *This restaurant must have a very clean kitchen.*
WAITER : Thank you, sir, but how did you know?
DINER : *Everything tastes of soap.*

Lemon
What do you give a hurt lemon?
Lemonade, of course.

Lettuce
*What's the difference between a mouldy lettuce and a dismal
song?*
One's bad salad and the other's a sad ballad.

Lies
I can't stop telling lies.
I don't believe you.

Lift
What did one lift say to the other lift?
I think I'm going down with something.

Light bulb
What would you do if you swallowed a light bulb?
Use a candle.

Lightning
Why does lightning shock people?
Because it doesn't know how to conduct itself.

Lobster
Why did the lobster blush?
Because the sea weed.

Madness
What do you call mad fleas?
Loony ticks.

Magician
What do you call a space magician?
A flying saucerer.

Manners
The very fat woman turned to the man sitting next to her in
    the bus and said in a loud voice:
'*If you were a gentleman, you'd stand up and let one of
    those women sit down.*'
'And if you were a lady,' said the man, 'you'd get up and
    let all four of them sit down.'

Mathematics
If two's company and three's a crowd, what is four and five?
Nine.

Meanness
Who is the meanest man in the world?
The man who finds a crutch, then breaks his leg so that he can use it.

Meat
WAITER: *And how did you find the meat, sir?*
CUSTOMER: Oh, I just lifted up a chip and there it was.

Medicine
DOCTOR: *Did you drink your medicine after your bath?*
PATIENT: After drinking the bath I didn't have too much room for the medicine.

Memory
PATIENT: *Doctor, Doctor, I've lost my memory.*
DOCTOR: When did this happen?
PATIENT: *When did what happen?*

Metal
Did you hear about the man who ate little bits of metal all day?
It was his staple diet.

Metronome
What is a metronome?
A dwarf in the Paris underground.

Minimum
What's the definition of minimum?
A very small mother.

Moses
How do we know that Moses wore a wig?
Because sometimes he was seen with Aaron and sometimes
  without.

Motherhood
A very proud mother phoned up a big Sunday newspaper
and reported that she'd given birth to seventeen children.
The girl at the desk didn't quite catch the message and
asked: 'Would you repeat that?'
  'Not if I can help it,' the woman replied.

Motorbike
What kind of motorbike can cook eggs?
A scrambler.

Mouse
What is the largest species of mouse in the world?
A hippopotamouse.

Musician
*Did you hear about the musician who spent all his time in
  bed?*
Yes, he wrote sheet music.

Nailbiting
MAN: *At last I've cured my son of biting his nails.*
FRIEND: Really? How did you manage that?
MAN: *Knocked all his teeth out.*

Napoleon
Where did Napoleon keep his armies?
Up his sleevies.

Nationality
What nationality are you?
Well, my mother was born in Iceland and my father was

33

born in Cuba so I suppose that makes me an ice cube.

Newsagent
Have you heard the one about the man who bought a paper shop? It blew away.

Nightwatchman
What's the difference between a nightwatchman and a butcher?
One stays awake and the other weighs a steak.

Noah's Ark
Why didn't the two worms go into Noah's ark in an apple?
Because everyone had to go in pairs.

Nuts
WOMAN IN A GREENGROCER'S : One pound of mixed nuts and not too many coconuts, please.

Octopus
What do you call a neurotic octopus?
A crazy, mixed-up squid.

Oil
Which animals have to be oiled?
Mice, because they squeak.

Oranges
An orange went to telephone a friend but the other orange didn't give her the message. Why?
Because the pips went.

Owl
What did the owl and the goat do at the square dance?
The hootenanny.

Oxygen
TEACHER: *If we breath oxygen in the daytime, what do we breathe at night?*
PUPIL: Nitrogen?

Paint
PSYCHIATRIST: *And what seems to be the trouble?*
PATIENT: Well, doctor, I keep having this tremendous urge to paint myself all over with gold paint.
PSYCHIATRIST: *You are suffering from a gilt complex.*

Painting
What did the oil painting say to the wall?
First they framed me, then they hung me.

Pancakes
CUSTOMER: *Waiter, will the pancakes be long?*
WAITER: No, sir, round.

Party
How would you describe a party at a camping site?
Intense excitement.

Peach

DRINKER : *Excuse me, do you know how to make a fresh peach punch?*

BARMAN : Sure – give her boxing lessons.

Pen

PATIENT : *Doctor, Doctor, what can I do? My little boy has swallowed my pen.*

DOCTOR : Use a pencil till I get there.

Pencil

Shall I tell you the joke about the pencil?
No, there's no point in it.

Piano

PIANO TUNER : *I've come to tune your piano.*

MAN : But we didn't send for you.

TUNER : *No, but your neighbours did.*

Piglets

Why didn't the piglets listen to their father?
Because he was such a boar.

Pigs
What do you call a stupid pig thief?
A hamburglar.

Plumber
What vegetable needs a plumber?
A leek.

Pocket calculator
Would you like to buy a pocket calculator, sir?
No thanks, I know how many pockets I've got.

Police
What did the policeman say to the man with three heads?
' 'Allo, 'allo, 'allo.'

Pony
What do you give a pony with a cold?
Cough stirrup.

Pound note
PATIENT: *Doctor, Doctor, I feel like a pound note.*
DOCTOR: Go shopping – the change will do you good.

Prisoners
NEWSCASTER: Two prisoners escaped today. One is seven feet tall and the other is four feet six inches. Police are looking high and low for them.

Pudding
How do you start a milk pudding race?
Sago.

Punctuality
TEACHER: *You should have been here at nine o'clock.*
PUPIL: Why, what happened?

Puppetry
What's the best way to get into the puppetry business?
Pull a few strings.

Putt
What goes putt-putt-putt-putt?
A bad golfer.

Questions
What never asks questions but gets plenty of answers?
A doorbell.

Rain
It's raining cats and dogs today.
I know – I've just stepped into a poodle.

Reindeer
What do reindeer say before they tell you a joke?
This one will sleigh you.

Road
Why did the elephant cross the road?
Because it was the chicken's day off.

Robbery
What sort of robbery is the easiest?
A safe robbery.

Robin Hood
What did Little John say when Robin Hood fired at him?
That was an arrow escape.

Rock cakes
What do you do if somebody offers you a rock cake?
Take your pick.

Romance
'Darling, do you love me?' sighed Romeo.
'Of course I do,' sighed Juliet.
'Darling, whisper something soft and sweet in my ear.'
'Lemon meringue pie.'

Runner
Who was the fastest runner in history?
Adam. He was the first in the human race.

Sandwiches
What did the traffic warden have in his sandwiches?
Traffic jam.

Sausages

PATIENT: *Doctor, my family think I'm mad.*

DOCTOR: Why?

PATIENT: *Because I like sausages.*

DOCTOR: Nonsense, I like sausages too.

PATIENT: *You do? You must come round and see my collection. I have hundreds.*

Sheep

A man goes into a butcher's shop and says, 'Have you got a sheep's head?'

The butcher replies, 'No, it's just the way I part my hair.'

Sheep

PATIENT: *Doctor, I've just swallowed a sheep.*

DOCTOR: How do you feel?

PATIENT: *Very ba-a-a-ad.*

Shoes

What wears shoes, but has no feet?
The pavement.

Sleep

PATIENT: *Doctor, Doctor, I can't get to sleep at night.*

DOCTOR: Lie on the edge of the bed and you'll soon drop off.

Soccer

CAPTAIN: *Why didn't you stop the ball?*

GOALIE: What do you think the nets are for?

Soup

CUSTOMER: *Waiter, what soup is this?*

WAITER: It's bean soup, sir.

CUSTOMER: *I don't care what it was, I want to know what it is now.*

Spaceman
What do you call a crazy spaceman?
An astronut.

Spectacles
DOCTOR : *You need glasses.*
PATIENT : How did you know?
DOCTOR : *I could tell as soon as you walked through the window.*

Spelling
How do you spell 'Crocodile'?
K-r-o-k-o-d-i-a-l.
The dictionary spells it 'C-r-o-c-o-d-i-l-e.'
You didn't ask me how the dictionary spelt it.

Spies
What is the most common illness among spies?
A code in the nose.

Splinters
From which seafaring book can you get splinters?
A log-book.

Spoon
PATIENT : *Doctor, Doctor, I feel like a spoon.*
DOCTOR : Sit down and don't stir.

Spy
What do you call a frog spy?
A croak and dagger agent.

Stories
What do you call a pig who tells long, dull stories?
A big boar.

Streets
When are the streets most greasy?
When the rain is dripping.

Stupidity
What makes you think I'm so stupid?
Well, when you went to that mind-reader, she only charged
you half-price!

Sty
What do you call pigs who live together?
Pen friends.

Suit
I've just bought a suit that fits me like a glove – four trouser
legs and one sleeve.

Sunglasses
Have you heard the one about the man who always wore
sunglasses? He took a dim view of things.

Supper
What did the cannibal have for supper?
Baked beings on toast.

Swiss roll
How do you make a Swiss roll?
Push him off the top of an alp.

Teeth
What's got teeth but can't bite?
A comb.

Telegram
Why is it useless to send a telegram to Washington?
Because he's dead.

Theatre
Why is the theatre such a sad place?
The seats are always in tiers.

Time
How can you check the time without looking at your watch?
Eat an apple and count the pips.

Tin-openers
What dance do tin-openers do?
The Can-Can.

Tonsils
FIRST TONSIL: *What are you getting dressed up for?*
SECOND TONSIL: Oh, the doctor is taking me out tonight.

Tooth
How do you get through life with only one tooth?
You grin and bare it.

Tower of Pisa
What makes the Tower of Pisa lean?
A strict diet.

Traffic lights
What did the traffic lights say to the sports car?
Don't look now, I'm changing.

Train driver
What's the difference between a train driver and a teacher?
One minds the train and the other trains the mind.

Travel
How long is the next bus?
Oh, about six metres.

Twig
CUSTOMER : *Waiter, there's a twig in my soup.*
WAITER :   Hold on, sir, I'll call the branch manager.

Twins
What language do twins speak in Holland?
Double Dutch.

Umbrella
When should a mouse carry an umbrella?
When it's raining cats and dogs.

Vampires
What dance do vampires do?
The Fangdango.

Vegetarian
Did you hear about the vegetarian cannibal? He would
only eat Swedes.

Vegetarian
Why did the cannibal become a vegetarian?
Well, you can go off people, you know.

Vikings
What did Vikings use for secret messages?
The Norse Code.

Volcano
What's the definition of a volcano?
A mountain with a hiccup.

Volkswagens
Where do Volkswagens go when they get old?
The Old Volks Home.

Waiter
CUSTOMER : *There's only one piece of meat on my plate.*
WAITER :   Wait a minute, sir, and I'll cut it in two.

Watch
What does your watch say?
'Tick, tock!'

Water
When is water musical?
When it's piping hot.

Water otter
What is the proper name for a water otter?
A kettle.

Week
Who invented the five-day-week?
Robinson Crusoe. He had all his work done by Friday.

Weight
What's a good way of putting on weight?
Eat a peach, swallow the centre, and you've gained a stone.

Whales
Where do you weigh whales?
At a whale weigh station.

Window
Why did a man throw his watch out of the window?
To see time fly.

Winds
What did the south wind say to the north wind?
Let's play draughts.

Witch
What is the difference between a very small witch and a deer running from the hunter?
One is a stunted hag and the other a hunted stag.

Woodpecker
What do you get when you cross a carrier pigeon with a woodpecker?

A bird who knocks before he delivers his message.

Wool
What happened to the cat that ate a ball of wool?
It had mittens.

Worm
How can you tell which end of the worm is his head?
Tickle his middle and see which end smiles.

Yellow
What's yellow on the inside and green on the outside?
A banana disguised as a cucumber.

Zebra
What do you get if you cross a zebra with a pig?
Striped sausages.

Zebra crossing
POLICEMAN TO PEDESTRIAN: *Here! Why are you crossing the road in this dangerous spot – can't you see there's a zebra crossing only fifty yards away?*

PEDESTRIAN: Well, I hope it's having better luck than I am.

Animal Magic

FARMER: *What is the treatment for a pig with a sore throat?*
VET: You must apply this oinkment.

MOTHER: *Jane, have you given the goldfish fresh water today?*
JANE: No. They haven't finished what I gave them yesterday.

What did the croaking frog say to his friend?
I think I've got a person in my throat!

What would you get if you crossed a flea with a rabbit?
A bug's bunny.

JACK: *If your dog was chewing up your favourite book, what would you do?*
JILL: I'd take the words right out of his mouth.

How does an octopus go into battle?
Well armed!

JIM: *How is a skunk different from a rabbit?*
JOE: I don't know. How?
JIM: *The skunk uses a cheaper deodorant!*

Mrs Barker went along to the Battersea Dogs' Home to get a dog as a present for her little boy.

'Are you sure this mongrel will make a good pet?' she asked the keeper.

'Without a doubt, madam,' said the keeper. 'He'll make a wonderful pet. He'll eat anything and he's especially fond of children.'

BLACK SHEEP: *Baa-a-a-a-a-a.*
WHITE SHEEP: Moo!
BLACK SHEEP: *What do you mean, 'Moo'?*
WHITE SHEEP: I'm learning a foreign language.

What should you do if you wake up in the middle of the night and hear a mouse squeaking?
Oil it!

BILL: *What kind of dog is that?*
BEN: He's a police dog.
BILL: *He doesn't look much like a police dog to me.*
BEN: Of course not: he's a plain clothes police dog!

LITTLE BOY BLUE: *Baa, baa, black sheep, have you any wool?*
BLACK SHEEP: What do you think this is, you nitwit, nylon?

DICK: *Tom has been sent to prison for stealing a pig.*
HARRY: How could they prove that he did it?
DICK: *The pig squealed!*

If you feed a cow pound notes what will you get?
Rich milk.

A man went to an animal auction not long ago and found just what he wanted. It was a beautiful African parrot and the man decided to bid for it. The bids went higher and higher, but finally the man managed to get the bird for £699, the highest price ever paid for an African parrot in an animal auction. As soon as he had bought the bird, the man suddenly remembered that he had forgotten to find out the most important thing about the parrot.

'Does the parrot talk?' he asked the auctioneer anxiously.

'Who do you think was bidding against you all the time?' was the auctioneer's reply.

Best-sellers

According to the latest figures supplied by bookshops throughout the world, these are the twenty best-selling titles of all time:

1 The Greatest Detective Stories Ever *by Watts E. Dunn*

2 Silence is Golden *by Xavier Breth*

3 How I Won the Pools *by Jack Potts*

4 Parachute Jumping *by Hugo Furst*

5 How Not to Shoot Your Wife *by Mr Completely*

6 The Joys of Hitchhiking *by Marsha Long*

7 What's Up, Doc? *by Howie Dewin*

8 Who Killed Cock Robin? *by Howard I. Know*

9 The Art of Button-Collecting *by Zipporah Broaken*

10 How to Fall Out of the Window *by Eileen Dover*

11 Why You Need Insurance *by Justin Case*

12 Monster-Making as a Hobby *by Frank N. Stine*

13 My Life in a Lunatic Asylum *by I. M. Nutty*

14 Around the Mountain *by Sheila B. Cumming*

15 Peek-a-Boo *by I. C. Hugh*

16 Neck Exercise *by G. Rarff*

17 How to Make an Igloo *by S. K. Mow*

18 Outsize Clothes *by L. E. Fant*

19 How to Diet *by M. T. Cupboard*

20 The Pleasures of Horse-Riding *by Jim Karna*

Cross-Breeding

What do you get if you cross a round black hat with a rocket?
A very fast bowler.

What do you get if you cross a miserable man with a spaceship?
A moan-rocket.

What do you get if you cross a group of stars with a silver cup?
A constellation prize.

What do you get if you cross a space pistol, a cheer, and a hippopotamus?
A hip-hippo-ray gun.

What do you get if you cross the Moon with the top of a house?
A lun-attic.

What do you get if you cross two parts of the head, one treble-o, and Attila,

54

Ear-tooth-thousand and Hun (year 2001).

Daffinitions

Accord A thick piece of string

Acorn Something caused by a tight shoe

Address Something worn by girls and women

Adore Entrance to a house

Alphabet soup Eating your own words

Bachelor A man who never Mrs anyone

Bandleader Someone who has to face the music

Bathing beauty A girl worth wading for

Bird house Home tweet home

Blockhead A person who gets splinters every time he
  scratches his head.

Cannibal A person who is fed up with people

Castor oil A lubricant for fishing rods

Celery What you get for working

Coconut Someone who is crazy about hot chocolate

Conceit A case of 'I' strain

Denial The main river of Egypt

Diet A triumph of mind over platter

Divine What the grapes grow on

Drill Sergeant An army dentist

Dumbwaiter Someone who can't get your order right

Eclipse What a gardener does to a hedge

Engineers What engines hear with

Entrance Be in a deep hypnotic state

Everest The laziest mountain in the world

Explain Eggs cooked without any trimmings

Fireman Someone who ought to go to blazes

Fission An atomic scientist's favourite food

Flying saucer A dish that is out of this world

Foul language What you hear if you pass near the chicken coop

Free speech When you can use someone else's phone

Garden hose Socks worn while you work in the garden

Ghost writer A spooksman

Giraffe The highest form of animal life

Goose A bird that grows down as it grows up

Gross ignorance 144 times worse than ordinary ignorance

Half a loaf A short holiday

Half-wit Someone who spends half his time being funny

Hatchet What a hen does with an egg

Hollow An empty greeting

Horse doctor A physician with a sore throat

Ice Skid stuff

Ice cream Yell at the top of your voice

Icicle An eavesdropper

Illegal A sick bird

Indistinct Where you put the dirty dishes

Jack-in-the-box An open and shut case

Jargon A missing container

Jet-setter A fast-flying dog

Jitterbug A nervous insect

Jonah The strongest man in the Bible. Even a whale could not keep him down

Kidnap What a small child often does after lunch

Kindred An abnormal fear of relatives

Knob A thing to adore

Launch A meal for astronauts

Lazy bones A skeleton that doesn't like to work

Leopard An animal easy to spot

Library The tallest building in the world because it has the most stories

Lisp When you call a spade a thpade

Mayor A female horse

Meow A catty remark

Mistake A woman shoplifter

Moonbeams What holds the moon up

Mushroom The place where they serve the school food

Nightingale Very windy evening

Nightmare A horse that keeps late hours

Noise A cause of earitation

Noodle soup Nourishment for the brain

Normalise Good vision

Occur A mongrel dog

Ohm There is no place like it

Open house Home without a roof

Ouch The sound heard when two porcupines kiss

Out-of-bounds An elderly kangaroo

Pasteurise Beyond what you can see

Peephole Members of the human race

Piano chord What you tie a piano up with

Pillow Headquarters

Playpen A writing device used by dramatists

Quack A doctor who treats sick ducks

Quadruplets Four crying out loud

Quartz There are four to a gallon

Ragtime When your clothes wear out

Refuse What must be done when all the lights in the house go out

Relief What trees do each spring

River bank Where fish keep their money

Robin A bird that steals

School spirit Ghost that haunts a school

Seashell A torpedo

Short cut A small wound

Snack A refresher course

Sourpuss A cat that has swallowed a lemon

Temper The only thing you can lose and still have

Tortoise What the teacher did

Treason The male offspring of a tree

Unaware What you put on first and take off last

Undercover agent A spy in bed

Underground garage A wall-to-wall car pit

Unit A term of abuse

Urchin The lower part of a woman's face

Vicious circle A round geometric figure with a nasty temper

Volcano A mountain that has blown its stack

Volga boatman A coarse seaman

Watchmaker Someone who works overtime

Wheeler dealer A cartyre salesman

Witchcraft A flying broomstick

Woe The opposite of 'giddyup'

Wristwatch A clock for people who don't like time on their hands

X What hens lay

X-ray Bellyvision

Yank A dentist of American extraction

Yardstick Something that has three feet but can't walk

Yearnings What you receive for working

Zebra A horse with venetian blinds

Zing What you do with a zong

Zoo A place where people go and animals are barred

Epilaughs

These three epitaphs are taken from actual gravestones found in the United Kingdom:

'Here snug in grave my wife doth lie;
Now she's at rest and so am I!'

'Here lie the bones of Richard Lawton,
Whose death, alas! was strangely brought on.
Trying one day his corns to mow off,
The razor slipped and cut his toe off;
His toe, or rather what it grew to,
An inflammation quickly flew to,
Which took alas to mortifying,
And was the cause of Richard's dying.'

'Here lie I,
Bereft of breath,
Because a cough
Carried me off;
Then a coffin
They carried me off in.'

Family Fun

MOTHER: *Come in, Darren, and I'll give you some chocolate biscuits. Are your feet dirty?*
DARREN: Yes, Mum, but I've got my shoes on.

MOTHER: *You behaved very nicely in church today, dear.*
DAUGHTER: Yes, when that nice man offered me a whole plate of money I said, 'No, thank you.'

JACK: *My grandfather has a wooden leg.*
JILL: That's nothing, my grandmother has a cedar chest.

SON: *Dad, what is a weapon?*
DAD: It's something you fight with.
SON: *Is mother your weapon?*

HUSBAND: *My wife treats me like an idol.*
FRIEND: Why do you say that?
HUSBAND: *She feeds me burnt offerings at every meal.*

LITTLE WILLIE: *Mummy, do you remember that special plate you always worried I would break?*
MOTHER: Yes, what about it?
LITTLE WILLIE: *Well, your worries are over!*

A grandfather took his young grandson to the opera for the very first time as a special treat. The conductor began to wave his baton and the soprano started to sing her famous aria. The boy was fascinated by everything he saw and heard, but eventually he turned to his grandfather and asked, 'Why is he hitting her with his stick?'

'He's not hitting her,' answered the grandfather with a smile.

'Well, if he's not hitting her, why is she screaming?'

Little Willie rushed out of the bathroom. 'Oh, Mum,' he cried, 'I've just seen something running across the bathroom floor with no legs!'

'Nonsense, dear. What on earth are you talking about?'

'Water!'

Grub's up

Here's a glorious gaggle of gags for greedy guzzlers.

What did the fat man say when he sat down to eat his dinner?
I'm afraid this food is all going to waist.

JULIET: *May I have a fried egg?*
MOTHER: With pleasure.
JULIET: *No, with chips!*

MOTHER: *If you eat any more of that pie, you'll burst.*
LITTLE WILLIE: Okay, Mum – just pass the pie and get out of the way.

TOM: *Mum made an awful mistake today and gave Dad soap flakes instead of cornflakes for breakfast!*
DICK: Was he angry?
TOM: *He foamed at the mouth!*

MOTHER: *Eat your spinach, dear. It will put colour into your cheeks.*
JOHNNY: Who wants green cheeks?

Howlers

We all make mistakes. Among the most entertaining mistakes are the ones we make at school. Here are fifty classic schoolroom howlers to prove the point.

1 Antimony is money inherited from your mother's aunt.

2 Cosmic rays are electric treatment to make women beautiful.

3 Philatelists were a race of people who lived in Biblical times.

4 All people were petrified in the Stone Age.

5 Socrates died from an overdose of wedlock.

6 Austerity is an old religion but today even politicians teach it.

7 Blood consists of red corkscrews and white corkscrews.

8 Jacob had a brother called Seesaw.

9 Ladies who sing low kind of songs are called contraltos.

10 A trombone is an instrument you play by pulling it in and out.

11 The Gorgons had long snakes in their hair. They looked like women only more horrible.

12 Poetry is when every line starts with a capital letter.

13 When a dog has puppies it is called a litre.

14 An oxygen has eight sides.

15 Euthenasia is the eastern part of Asia.

16 All Mormons are polygons.

17 The Merchant of Venice was a famous Italian who bought and sold canal boats.

18 When a man is married to one woman it is called monotony.

19 Kubla Khan is a black secret society wearing white night shirts.

20 Homer wrote *The Oddity*.

21 A convoy is a collection of small birds like cartridges.

22 Herrings go about the sea in shawls.

23 Reefs are what you put on coffins.

24 Pegasus is a hobby horse used by carpenters.

25 Soviet is another name for a table napkin.

26 Letters in sloping type are called hysterics.

27 A blizzard is the inside of a chicken.

28 A ruminating animal chews its cubs.

29 Mushrooms look like umbrellas because they grow where it's wet.

30 A centimetre is an insect with a hundred legs.

31 The future of 'I give' is 'You take'.

32 The vowels are: a, e, i, o, u, and sometimes w and y.

33 The passive verb is when the subject is the sufferer, as 'I am loved'.

34 A metaphor is a suppressed smile.

35 Water is composed of Oxygin and Hydrogin. Oxygin is pure but Hydrogin is gin and water.

36 There are four elements, mustard, salt, pepper and vinegar, although I think vinegar is really an acid.

37 A good cosmetic is salt and water. Cosmetics make you sick.

38 Handel was a little boy in a tale with his sister called *Handel and Grettal*.

39 Tom Sawyer was a smart boy, his character was always good sometimes.

40 The appendix is a part of the book for which nobody has found much use.

41 'The child is father to the man'. This was written by Shakespeare. He didn't often make that kind of mistake.

42 Marshal Goering was a fat man because he was one of Hitler's stoutest supporters.

43 Washington was a great general who always began a battle with the fixed determination to win or lose.

44 Dusk is little bits of fluff you find under the bed.

45 Necessity is the mother of convention.

46 A graven image is a nice grave stone.

47 Income is a yearly tax.

48 A surname is the name of somebody you say 'Sir' to.

49 Faith is believing what you know is untrue.

50 Ambiguity is telling the truth when you don't mean to.

It pays to advertise

Sign on a travel agency window:
PLEASE GO AWAY

Sign at a butcher's shop:
HONEST SCALES – NO TWO WEIGHS ABOUT IT

Sign outside a laundry:
WE'LL CLEAN FOR YOU, WE'LL PRESS FOR YOU,
WE'LL EVEN DYE FOR YOU

Sign on a bird's cage in a pet shop:
FOR SALE – CHEEP

Sign outside a hotel:
WANTED – HOTEL WORKERS: ONLY
INEXPERIENCED NEED APPLY

Sign at a tyre depot:
WE SKID YOU NOT

Sign outside a shoe shop:
COME IN AND HAVE A FIT

Sign outside a funeral directors:
SATISFACTION GUARANTEED OR YOUR
MUMMY BACK

Joking on the job

FIRST GARDENER : *I used to work with thousands under me.*
SECOND GARDENER :   Really?
FIRST GARDENER : *Yes, I cut the grass in a cemetery!*

TOM : *Did you hear about the angel who lost his job?*
DICK : No, what happened?
TOM : *He had harp failure.*

TIM : *My dad makes faces all day.*
TOM : Why does he do that?
TIM : *Because he works in a clock factory!*

The site foreman had ten very lazy labourers working for him, so he decided to try to trick them into doing some work.

'I've got a nice easy job today for the laziest man here,' he said. 'Will the laziest man please put up his hand.'

Nine hands went up.

'Why didn't you put your hand up?' he asked the tenth man.

'Too much trouble,' was the reply.

PRISONER : *The judge sent me here for the rest of my life.*
PRISON GOVERNOR : Got any complaints?
PRISONER : *Do you call breaking rocks with a hammer* rest?

What sort of children does a florist have?
Blooming idiots!

CHEF: *What is the best thing to put in a pie?*
TRAINEE: Your teeth!

CUSTOMER IN A HURRY: *Give me a mousetrap quickly, please. I've only two minutes to catch a train.*
SHOP ASSISTANT: Sorry, we don't have any that big!

JACK: *I hear the men are striking.*
JILL: What for?
JACK: *Shorter hours.*
JILL: Good for them. I've always thought sixty minutes was too long for an hour.

CONDUCTOR: *Will you please open the piano?*
PIANIST: I can't. The keys are on the inside!

JACK: *Did you hear what the burglar gave his wife for her birthday?*
JILL: No, what?
JACK: *A stole.*

Knock Knock knonsense

A
Knock Knock
Who's there?

Ammonia.
Ammonia who?
Ammonia a bird in a gilded cage.

B

Knock Knock
Who's there?
Barbara.
Barbara who?
'Barbara black sheep, have you any wool . . . ?'

C

Knock Knock
Who's there?
Cereal.
Cereal who?
Cereal pleasure to meet you.

D

Knock Knock
Who's there?
Dawn.
Dawn who?
Dawn do anything I wouldn't do.

E

Knock Knock
Who's there?
Earl.
Earl who?
Earl be glad to tell you if you open the door.

F

Knock Knock
Who's there?

Felix.
Felix who?
Felix-cited all over.

G
Knock Knock
Who's there?
Guinevere.
Guinevere who?
Guinevere going to get together?

H
Knock Knock
Who's there?
Hiram.
Hiram who?
Hiram fine, how are you?

I
Knock Knock
Who's there?
Ina Claire.
Ina Claire who?
'Ina Claire day, you can see forever . . .'

J
Knock Knock
Who's there?
Joan.
Joan who?
Joan call us, we'll call you.

K
Knock Knock

Who's there?
Kent.
Kent who?
Kent you tell who it is?

L
Knock Knock
Who's there?
Lucinda.
Lucinda who?
'Lucinda sky with diamonds . . .'

M
Knock Knock
Who's there?
Myth.
Myth who?
Myth you, too.

N
Knock Knock
Who's there?
Noah.
Noah who?
Noah don't know who you are either.

O
Knock Knock
Who's there?
Olive.
Olive who?
Olive you too, honey.

P

Knock Knock
Who's there?
Police.
Police who?
Police open the door.

Q

Knock Knock
Who's there?
Quebec.
Quebec who?
Quebec to the end of the line.

R

Knock Knock
Who's there?
Roland.
Roland who?
Roland stone gathers no moss.

S

Knock Knock
Who's there?
Sarah.
Sarah who?
Sarah doctor in the house?

T

Knock Knock
Who's there?
Tennis.
Tennis who?
Tennis five plus five.

U

Knock Knock
Who's there?
Utica.
Utica who?
Utica high road and I'll take the low road.

V

Knock Knock
Who's there?
Viola.
Viola who?
Viola sudden you don't know me?

W

Knock Knock
Who's there?
Wicked.
Wicked who?
Wicked make beautiful music together.

X

Knock Knock
Who's there?
Xavier.
Xavier who?
Xavier breath! I'm not leaving.

Y

Knock Knock
Who's there?
Yoga.
Yoga who?
Yoga what it takes!

Z

Knock Knock
Who's there?
Zaul.
Zaul who?
Zaul there is and there ain't no more.

Lear's limericks

Edward Lear died on 29th January 1888 at the age of 75,
but his nonsense will live for ever. He didn't invent the
limerick, but he made it world-famous. In his lifetime he
wrote hundreds of limericks, and here are five firm
favourites:

There was a Young Lady of Dorking,
Who bought a large bonnet for walking;
But its colour and size so bedazzled her eyes
That she very soon went back to Dorking.

There was an Old Man with a nose,
Who said, 'If you choose to suppose
That my nose is too long, you are certainly wrong!'
That remarkable Man with a nose.

There was a Young Lady whose nose
Was so long that it reached to her toes;
So she hired an Old Lady, whose conduct was steady,
To carry that wonderful nose.

There was an Old Man who said, 'Hush!
I perceive a young bird in this bush!'
When they said – 'Is it small?' He replied – 'Not at all!
It is four times as big as the bush!'

There was a Young Lady whose chin
Resembled the point of a pin;
So she had it made sharp, and purchased a harp,
and played several tunes with her chin.

Motoring madness

A motorist was driving down a one-way street the wrong
way. He was stopped by a policeman on a motorbike.
POLICEMAN: *Do you know where you're going?*
DRIVER: Yes, but I must be very late. Everyone else is
coming back!'

What kind of song do you sing in a car?
A cartoon!

What kind of driver never gets arrested?
A screwdriver.

What part of the car is the cause of most accidents?
The nut that holds the wheel!

What is an autobiography?
The life story of an automobile

TOM : *People complain about backseat drivers, but I have to say that I've been driving all my life and I've never heard a word from the back seat.*
DICK : What kind of car do you drive?
TOM : *A hearse!*

What age is most important?
Mileage!

GARAGE MECHANIC : *Is your horn broken?*
MOTORIST : No, it doesn't care.
GARAGE MECHANIC : *What do you mean?*
MOTORIST : It doesn't give a hoot!

Sign in a factory where they make mini cars:
THINK BIG – AND YOU'RE FIRED!

News flash

The marriage of the two lighthouse keepers was said last night to be on the rocks ...

The Chancellor of the Exchequer announced today that under a new pay award scheme barbers are to get more fringe benefits ...

Last night a large hole was made in the forty foot high fence surrounding the Broadstairs' Nudist Camp. Police are now looking into it ...

Owing to a strike at the Meteorological Office, there will be no weather tomorrow ...

The Common Market Commissioners' plan to have all meat pies wrapped in tin has been foiled ...

Marmaduke Mustard, the recently elected Member of Parliament for Puddlecombe, took his seat in the House of Commons this morning – but he was forced to put it back.

One hundred tonnes of human hair was stolen last night from a wig factory in Scunthorpe. Police are combing the area . . .

The Chairman of the British Periscope Manufacturers' Association said last night that business was looking up . . .

Odd ode

A boy who swims may say he swum,
But milk is skimmed and seldom skum,
And nails you trim, they are not trum.
When words you speak, these words are spoken,
But a nose is tweaked and can't be twoken,
And what you seek is seldom soken.
If we forget then we've forgotten,
But things we wet are never wotten,
And houses let cannot be lotten.
The goods one sells are always sold,
But fears dispelled are not dispold,
And what you smell is never smold.
When young, a top you oft saw spun,
But did you see a grin e'er grun,
Or a potato nearly skun?

Pun fun

INTERVIEWER : *Why have you called your new play 'The broken leg?'*
PLAYWRIGHT : Because it needs a strong cast!

ESTATE AGENT : *I have got the ideal house for you, sir. It really is perfect. It doesn't have a flaw.*
HOUSE BUYER : But what do you walk on?

Did you know that Prince Charles was a bit of a cry-baby when he was small? That's why they called him The Prince of Wails!

Why was the theatre sad?
Because the seats were all in tiers!

Did you hear about the bossy chicken that stopped on the railway track? She wanted to lay it on the line!

JACK: *My father can play the piano by ear.*
JILL: That's nothing! My father fiddles with his whiskers!

TOM: *Who was Snow White's brother?*
DICK: Egg White!
HARRY: *I don't get the yolk!*

What did the adding machine say to the cashier?
You can count on me!

JACK: *Did you hear what the sea said to the beach?*
JILL: I'm not shore.
JACK: *No. The sea didn't say anything. It just waved!*

TOM : *Tell me, Dick, why do you always sleep in that oil tank?*

DICK : Because I like to get up oily in the morning!

There were two buckets sitting in the kitchen cupboard chatting to one another.

'You don't look like a well bucket,' said one.

'You're quite right,' replied the other, 'I am a little pail!'

Quick questions

1 If a plug doesn't fit, do you socket?

2 Does fishing result in net profits?

3 Is a budget a baby budgerigar?

4 If you cross a cat with a ball of wool, will you get mittens?

5 Is the Lord Privy Seal a noble animal rather like a sealion who lives in a lavatory?

Ridiculous riddles

When the orange wanted to fight the banana, why did the banana run away?
Because it was yellow.

Which fish go to heaven when they die?
Angel fish.

What did the old man do when he thought he was dying?
He moved into the living room.

Where do butterflies go to dance?
Moth balls.

Why did the scientist take a ruler to bed?
To see how long he slept.

What do you call a baby whale that's crying?
A little blubber.

Why does a rooster watch TV?
For hentertainment.

Why did the hero refuse to die for his lady love?
Because his was an undying love.

How does one get on to something in which there's a lot of money?
Climb on to the roof of a bank.

Why are manicurists always so wealthy?
Because they make money hand over fist.

Why did the boy wear two suits to the fancy dress party?
He went as twins.

What does a hard-working gardener always grow?
Tired.

Why is a belt like a dustcart?
Because it goes round and gathers the waist.

What's more dangerous than being with a fool?
Fooling with a bee.

Why did the girl put her hands in the alphabet soup?
Because she was groping for words.

From a medical point of view, why is a pig unique?
Because you kill him before you cure him.

Why did the man have a high-pitched voice and funny teeth?
Because he had a falsetto voice and a false set o' teeth.

Why was the doctor who fell into a well a fool?
Because he should have attended the sick and left the well alone.

Why is a squeaky shoe a great composer?
Because it has music in its sole.

What is the cheapest way to get to China?
Be born there.

Why do white sheep eat more than black ones?
Because there are more white sheep in the world.

Why is an empty matchbox the best matchbox?
Because it is matchless.

Why do we buy clothes?
Because we can't get them for nothing.

If a man smashed a clock, could he be accused of killing time?
Not if the clock struck first.

When is a shaggy dog most likely to enter your house?
When the door's open.

What is striped and goes round and round?
A zebra caught in a revolving door.

What is always behind time?
The back of a watch.

Why did the dishonest man grow a beard?
So no one could call him a bare-faced liar.

Which horses have their eyes nearest together?
The smallest horses.

Why can't a man marry his widow's sister?
Because he'd be dead.

What is a myth?
A lady with a lisp but no husband.

How can you avoid falling hair?
Jump out of the way.

Why couldn't the boy sleep in class?
Because the teacher talked too loudly.

What would happen if you crossed a chicken with a poodle?
The chicken would lay pooched eggs.

What are the three nicest nuts in the world?
Walnuts, peanuts and forget-me-nuts.

What's the difference between a milkmaid and a seagull?
One skims milk and the other skims water.

How do you know that a sausage doesn't like being fried?
Because it spits.

What did the piece of wood say to the electric drill?
You bore me.

Why did the poor dog chase his own tail?
He was trying to make both ends meet.

Why was the sick boy about to croak?
Because he swallowed a frog.

How can you stop a rooster from crowing on Sunday?
Eat him on Saturday.

Why didn't the piglets listen to their father?
Because he was a boar.

What bow cannot be tied?
A rainbow.

If you had fifteen cows and four goats, what would you have?
Plenty of milk.

Why was the farmer cross?
Someone had walked on his corn.

What can run and whistle – but can't walk or talk?
A locomotive.

What's the most intelligent insect you'll meet at school?
A spelling bee.

What falls but never gets hurt?
Snow.

*Which takes less time to get ready for a trip: an elephant
or a rooster?*
A rooster, because he only takes his comb, while the
elephant has to take a whole trunk.

What country is useful at mealtimes?
China.

Science spot

Why did the germ cross the microscope?
To get to the other slide.

TOP SCIENTIST : *What does HNO3 stand for?*
YOUNG SCIENTIST : HNO3? Let me think now ... I'm sure
I know. It's on the tip of my tongue ...
TOP SCIENTIST : *Well, spit it out at once then! It's Nitric
Acid!*

Did you know that if you swallowed Uranium you would
certainly get atomic ache?

SCIENTIST : *I have just made an incredible discovery: how
to make wool out of milk.*
FRIEND : That certainly is extraordinary, but I'm afraid it
will make the cow feel a little sheepish!

SCIENCE TEACHER: *Name a liquid that cannot freeze.*
PUPIL: Hot water.

SCIENCE TEACHER: *Light travels at the rate of 186,000 miles per second. Don't you think that's remarkable?*
PUPIL: Not really. It's downhill all the way.

TOP SCIENTIST: *This gas is a deadly poison. What steps would you take if it escaped?*
YOUNG SCIENTIST: Large ones, sir!

Teacher's pet

ANGRY TEACHER: *Why are you so late?*
LAZY PUPIL: Well, I saw the sign in the street that said 'School ahead – go slow!'

ANGRY TEACHER: *I asked you to write a proper essay on the subject of milk, and you have only written two lines when I expected at least two pages. Why?*
PUPIL: I wrote about condensed milk.

TEACHER: *What was the Romans' most remarkable achievement?*
PUPIL: Learning Latin!

HISTORY TEACHER: *Why were the Dark Ages so called?*
PUPIL: Because they had so many knights!

Did you hear about the cross-eyed teacher who couldn't control his pupils?

SCIENCE TEACHER: *What is usually used as a conductor of electricity?*
WILLIE: Why, er ...
SCIENCE TEACHER: *Wire is correct. Now can you tell me what is the unit of electrical power?*
WILLIE: The what?
SCIENCE TEACHER: *The watt is quite right. Well done, Willie!*

ANGRY PUPIL: *I don't think I deserve nought for this work!*
GRINNING TEACHER: Neither do I, but it's the lowest mark I can give you.

ART TEACHER: *I asked you to draw a pony and trap. You have only drawn the pony.*
ART STUDENT: I thought the pony could draw the trap!

TEACHER: *Willie, what is a cannibal?*
WILLIE: I don't know.
TEACHER: *Well, if you ate your mother and father what would you be then?*
WILLIE: An orphan.

SCIENCE TEACHER: *What is an atom?*
PUPIL: The man who lived in the Garden of Eden with Eve.

TEACHER: *Now, Sally, tell me how many fingers you have.*

SALLY: Ten.

TEACHER: *If you lost four of them in an accident, what would you have then?*

SALLY: No more piano lessons!

JACK: *What is your favourite subject at school?*

JILL: Gozinta.

JACK: *Is that some kind of new language?*

JILL: No, it's just gozinta. You know, two gozinta four, four gozinta eight, eight gozinta sixteen . . .

TEACHER: *Can anyone in the class use 'fascinate' in a sentence?*

LITTLE WILLIE: I can, Miss.

TEACHER: *All right, Willie. Go ahead.*

LITTLE WILLIE: My duffle coat has ten buttons, but I can only fasten eight.

Under doctor's orders

Why do doctors and nurses wear masks?
So that if someone makes a mistake, no one will know who did it!

DOCTOR: *Are you still taking the cough medicine I gave you?*
PATIENT: No. I tasted it once and decided that I'd rather have the cough.

Once upon a time there was a country doctor who had to visit a patient in a small village. When he arrived at the patient's house, he was interested to see a deep well in the garden. He walked over to the well, but unfortunately tripped just as he reached it, fell into the well and was killed. The moral of this story is simple: Doctors should tend the sick and leave the well alone!

DOCTOR: *Have your eyes ever been checked?*
PATIENT: No, they've always been blue.

PATIENT: *Doctor, will I be able to read when I get my new glasses?*
DOCTOR: You certainly will.
PATIENT: *Oh, that's marvellous. I never knew how to before.*

When is an operation funny?
When it leaves the patient in stitches.

DOCTOR: *What's your average weight?*
PATIENT: I have no idea.
DOCTOR: *Well, what do you think is the most you have ever weighed?*
PATIENT: I'd say about eleven stone.
DOCTOR: *Good. And what do you think is the least you have ever weighed?*
PATIENT: Six pounds, thirteen ounces.

What is the difference between a hill and a pill?
A hill is hard to get up. A pill is hard to get down.

MRS JOHNSON (on the telephone): *Doctor, doctor, my son has just swallowed a pen.*
DOCTOR: Don't panic. I'll be right over.
MRS JOHNSON: *What should I do meanwhile?*
DOCTOR: Use a pencil.

PATIENT: *This ointment makes my arm smart.*
DOCTOR: Why don't you try rubbing some on your head then?

Vituperation

Vituperation means something insulting – and you won't find many insults more insulting than these!

MRS SMITH: *Whenever I'm down in the dumps I get myself a new hat.*
MRS BROWN: Oh, so that's where you find them!

TOM: *People call you the wonder boy.*
DICK: Do they really?
TOM: *Yes, they just look at you and wonder.*

ROMEO: *You dance very well.*
JULIET: I wish I could say the same for you.
ROMEO: *You could if you were as big a liar as I am.*

JACK: *I throw myself into everything I undertake.*
JILL: Why don't you go and dig a very deep well?

JACK: *Our dog is just like one of the family.*
JILL: Really? Which one?

JACK: *I've changed my mind.*
JILL: I'm so pleased to hear it. Does the new one work any better?

JACK: *Do you feel just like a cup of tea?*
JILL: Oh, yes.
JACK: *I thought so. You look sloppy, wet and hot!*

MRS SMITH: *I'd love you to stay for the night, but I'm afraid you will have to make your own bed.*
MRS BROWN: Oh, I don't mind at all.
MRS SMITH: *Good. Here's a hammer, a saw, and some nails. You'll find the wood in the garage.*

ROMEO: *You remind me of the deep blue sea.*
JULIET: You mean I'm so romantic?
ROMEO: *No, you just make me feel sick.*

Dear Aunt Gussie,
I didn't really forget your birthday. In fact, I was going to send you a present. I had planned to buy you some new handkerchiefs, but I forgot the size of your nose.

Waiter! waiter!

CUSTOMER: *Waiter, this soup is poisonous.*
WAITER: Who told you?
CUSTOMER: *A little swallow.*

WAITER: *Would you like to try some idiot soup, sir?*
CUSTOMER: What's idiot soup?
WAITER: *Thick soup.*

CUSTOMER: *Waiter, I'm in a hurry. Will the pancackes be long?*
WAITER: No sir, round!

WAITER: *I have frogs' legs, sir.*
CUSTOMER: Don't tell me your troubles. Just bring me a bowl of soup.

CUSTOMER: *I can't eat this revolting food. Call the manager.*
WAITER: It's no use, sir. He can't eat it either.

WAITER: *We have practically everything on the menu, sir.*
CUSTOMER: So I see. Would you bring me a clean one, please?

This section has been censored!

Yarns

Yarns aren't jokes about balls of wool. They are jokes that are a little longer than the average.

Once upon a time a gorilla walked into a coffee bar and ordered a cup of coffee. The man behind the counter was utterly amazed to see a gorilla walk in and to hear one speak, but he brought the coffee right away.

The gorilla drank his coffee in silence and then handed the man a five pound note. The man didn't believe for a moment that the gorilla would know anything about money, so he only gave the gorilla back one pound in change.

'I hope you enjoyed the coffee,' the man said to the gorilla. 'We don't get many gorillas coming in here, you know.'

'At four pounds a cup of coffee,' said the gorilla, 'I'm not surprised.'

Once upon a time there was a lion who wanted to find out why the other animals in the jungle weren't as handsome and strong as he was.

First he asked a zebra. The zebra didn't know. Next he asked a hippopotamus. The hippopotamus didn't know.

Next he asked a giraffe. The giraffe didn't know. Next he asked a crocodile. The crocodile didn't know. Next he asked a rhinoceros. The rhinoceros didn't know. Finally the lion came across a little mouse. He looked down at the mouse and said, 'Tell me, mouse, why aren't you as handsome and as strong and as big and as beautiful as I am?'

The little mouse looked up at the lion and said, 'Well, I've not been very well lately.'

Once upon a time there was a pilot who had his own old-fashioned aeroplane. It had an open cockpit and the pilot would sit in the front and his passengers just behind him. One day he offered to take an elderly couple up in the aeroplane. They had never been in a plane before and were very excited.

'You will enjoy the flight,' said the pilot. 'But you must promise to be good and not do any backseat driving.'

The old couple got into the plane and sat behind the pilot. The pilot flew the plane up into the sky and flew around for about twenty minutes. When he landed he said to the old man, 'You did very well for your first flight. I didn't hear a word out of you.'

'That's right,' said the old man. 'It wasn't easy. I almost said something back there when my wife fell out.'

Once upon a time there were three Red Indian squaws. One of them sat outside her wigwam on a leopard skin. Another sat outside her wigwam on a doe skin. The third sat outside her wigwam on a hippopotamus skin. The squaw who was sitting on the leopard skin had just one son. The squaw on the doe skin had just one son too. But the third squaw, the one sitting on the hippopotamus skin, had twin boys. This all goes to prove that the squaw on the hippopotamus is equal to the sons of the squaws on the other two hides!

Once upon a time one of King Arthur's knights came rushing into an inn. There was a terrible storm raging. 'Can you lend me a horse?' the knight asked the innkeeper. 'I have lost my own horse but I must get back to the Court of King Arthur tonight.'

'Oh, Sir Knight,' said the innkeeper, 'alas I have no horse to lend you. The only animal I have is that big, old sheepdog in the corner there.'

'Splendid,' said the knight. 'I shall ride him.'

'Oh no, sir,' said the innkeeper, 'I wouldn't send a knight out on a dog like this!'

Zizz iz ze end

'Zizz is ze end' is what a Frenchman says when you tell him a terrible joke. Well, since this is the end of this unique collection of terrible jokes, here's a final thought to cheer you up if you're feeling sad that you've reached the end of this book.

Don't worry if your job is small
And your rewards are few.
Remember that the mighty oak
Was once a nut like you!

More Beaver Books

We hope you have enjoyed this Beaver Book. Here are some of the other titles:

More Crazy Jokes A Beaver original. There are 999 hilarious jokes in this collection – to rocket you into rollicking laughter! Compiled by Janet Rogers and illustrated by Robert Nixon

It Figures! A Beaver original. Did you know that you can make four 4s equal 64, add five odd numbers to make a total of 14, or multiply a three-digit number so the answer is the number repeated twice? This book is crammed with incredible calculations, tricks and games with numbers, to baffle and amaze your friends and keep you amused for hours. Written by Clive Dickinson and illustrated by Graham Thompson

Ghostly Laughter A Beaver original. The chief characters in this unusual collection of stories are ghosts with a difference – they are so eccentric and lovable they will make you laugh! Chosen by Barbara Ireson and illustrated by William Geldart, the stories are a hilarious and thrilling read for the nine-and-over age group

These and many other Beavers are available from your local bookshop or newsagent, or can be ordered direct from: Hamlyn Paperback Cash Sales, PO Box 11, Falmouth, Cornwall TR10 9EN. Send a cheque or postal order, made payable to the Hamlyn Publishing Group, for the price of the book plus postage at the following rates:

UK: 40p for the first book, 18p for the second book, and 13p for each additional book ordered to a maximum charge of £1.49;
BFPO and Eire: 40p for the first book, 18p for the second book, plus 13p per copy for the next 7 books and thereafter 7p per book;
OVERSEAS: 60p for the first book and 18p for each extra book.

New Beavers are published every month and if you would like the *Beaver Bulletin*, a newsletter which tells you about new books and gives a complete list of titles and prices, send a large stamped addressed envelope to:

Beaver Bulletin
The Hamlyn Group
Astronaut House
Feltham
Middlesex TW14 9AR

352706